VEGAN LIFESTYLE

A BEGINNER'S JOURNEY TO THE HEALTHIEST PLANT BASED DIET AND HOW TO MAKE THE TRANSISITION TO THE VEGAN WORLD

Table of Contents

INTRODUCTION

Congratulations on purchasing this book and thank you for doing so!

Before the modern age of processed foods began, most people ate fresh fruits and vegetables on a daily basis. The meat was not eaten daily, and when it was, it was accompanied by a healthy serving of vegetables. Indeed, in those days people understood the health benefits of plant foods, which is why children were often reminded to eat their greens. It was good advice. Those green vegetables are powerhouses of nutrition. They are loaded with not only vitamins and minerals, but vital enzymes and proteins as well.

While many people follow a plant-based diet to drop some weight, they simultaneously lower their cholesterol, balance their blood sugar, and even lower blood pressure by eliminating the meat, dairy, and processed foods. When you eliminate meat and dairy, you also reduce the risks of many types of cancers and other chronic diseases.

Remember that a plant based diet rarely relies on pre-packaged foods that are full of unknowable chemicals and many hidden animal-based products. Instead, the right plant-based diet uses nutrient dense whole foods that are combined to create delicious and well-balanced meals.

Improving your health is a powerful argument in favor of a plant-based diet, but there is also an environmental argument. In June of 2010, the United Nations issued a report that said that the world's greenhouse gas problem is related directly to the use of fossil fuels but pointed out that agriculture (particularly the raising of meat and dairy products) was an equally dangerous part of the problem.

The report only validated what others had been saying all along, and that is that the meat and dairy industries consume and burn tons of fossil fuels as they raise food crops for animals, grow the animals, transport meat and products over long distances, and harm the environment every step of the way. For example, some studies have indicated that animal-based agriculture is responsible for around 18% of all greenhouse gas production. It is pretty substantial when you also read that all of the world's forms of transportation create less than 14% of greenhouse emissions.

Additionally, one resource indicated that the U.S. Geological Survey determined that it can take up to 18,000 gallons of water to raise the amount of meat needed in a single hamburger patty!

So, the positive environmental impacts alone are a good reason to consider shifting away from commercially produced meats and dairy foods. If we eliminate industrial foods from our diet, we certainly shrink the size of our carbon footprint because we are not participating in the use of fossil fuels or wasting energy. Thank you for purchasing this book it is my sincere hope that it will answer all your questions on the vegan diet.

Enjoy the read!

Chapter1: What is a Vegetarian Diet?

From the name itself, the Vegetarian diet, of course, focuses on vegetables as the main source of food. This diet is free from the consumption of any meat that includes red meat, seafood, poultry or the flesh of other animals.

According to studies, "vegetarianism" may have started centuries ago. Some anthropologists believe that the early humans are more of gatherers than hunters (this is opposed to the belief of the Paleo diet) and ate food coming from plants. These researchers also believed that health problems started to arise when humans began eating meat.

However, the rise of the concept began to waiver, because of several myths or misconceptions as well as the effort that comes with the diet. Nutritional benefits were also questioned but were all put to rest when "Diet for a New America" was published by John Robbins on 1987. The book discussed the "horror" of factory farming, the dangers of meat-based diets and even the environmental consequences of animal agriculture.

The book restarted the vegetarian way and also introduced the term "vegan."

From the 1980s till the present time, this lifestyle is proven efficient and comes with numerous benefits if done properly.

Take note of this: The key to the Vegetarian diet is meeting all the nutritional needs of people (of all ages and situation) and follow a well-planned diet.

People have different reasons on why they would like to explore vegetarianism, some of the traditional ideas are respected for sentient (can feel or perceive things) life, others are motivated by religious beliefs and animal rights and others due to health reasons.

Whatever the reason may be, being vegetarian is a conscious effort for many and may open doors to a healthier lifestyle.

Benefits of the Vegetarian Diet Clinical studies show that a vegetarian diet does good to the body,

Here are some of these benefits:

- Small Body Weight – A study carried out by the Cancer Research UK on 22,000 meat eaters, fish eaters, vegetarians and vegan found out that meat eaters will continue to put on weight compared to vegetarians. The study also figured out that vegans put on even less weight as they grow older compared to vegetarians and meat eaters.
- Better cholesterol level – Scientists demonstrated that a vegetarian diet made up of specific plant foods are as effective as drug treatments when it comes to bringing down cholesterol levels. The diet consisted of a combination of nuts, soy proteins, viscous fiber such as oats and barley and a special margarine that contain plant sterols.

- Lower risk of developing cancer – Vegetarians are at a reduced risk of developing many different types of cancer compared to meat eaters.

How to Become Vegetarian

If you have decided to become vegetarian, you may make one giant leap into it and quit eating animal's cold-turkey. You may also opt to make a gradual change, and this works better for two reasons:

- A progressive change to vegetarianism is useful in making a permanent lifestyle change.

- Sudden changes in eating habits may have unpleasant consequences in the digestive system.

- Make the transition slow. Start by increasing the number of vegetables in your plate. Then, have an all-vegetarian meal once or twice a week.

- Make sure that your diet is varied. Play around with different vegetables and grains. Spice up meals with seasonings.

- If you wish to continue consuming dairy, choose low or nonfat dairy products.

- Do not eat more than three or four egg yolks per week.

- Plan when you go food shopping. Fat-free meat substitutes can ease the transition.

- Read the food labels when you shop. Frozen vegetables are fine. Canned beans and vegetables are okay, too especially when it comes to convenience.

- Know where the specialty stores are.

- When you eat out, ask the chef to substitute beans for meat in the entrée or stick with the salad bar. There are ethnic cuisines such as Indian,

Vietnamese, and Thai that offer an abundance of vegetarian options.

- To avoid this problem, add seaweed to the water when cooking dried beans. Seaweeds have enzymes that will help you digest beans.

What to use instead of Animal Products

- Meat substitutes in soups and stews
o Wheat gluten or seitan – Wheat gluten or seitan is available in natural foods or Asian store. It is made from wheat and has a meaty texture.

- Egg replacers (binders)
o Ener-G egg replacer or similar product – available in natural food stores
o One small banana for one egg – for cakes or pancakes
o 2 T cornstarch or arrowroot starch for one egg
o ¼ cup tofu for one egg – blend tofu until smooth using the liquid ingredients before they are added to the dry ingredients

- Dairy substitutes in cooking
o Soymilk
o Rice, coconut, almond and other nut milk
o Soy margarine
o Soy or almond yogurt
    o Soy sour cream

Myths and Facts about Vegetarian Diet, A lot of people, are now interested in a vegetarian diet. With this interest, however, many still question if the vegetarian or vegan diet is healthy.

Pitfalls of the Vegetarian Diet

As you adjust to becoming vegetarian, you will encounter some fairly common pitfalls. If your goal in being vegetarian is to lose weight and improve overall health, these pitfalls will be a hindrance.

- Bread and pasta products are also high in calories. Just because the food is meat-free, doesn't mean you can go ahead and indulge.

- Look for fortified foods and consider taking supplements.

- Look for reliable sources of vitamin B-12 especially if you will eliminate dairy. Long-term vitamin B-12 deficiency can lead to anemia and permanent nerve or neurological damage. Sunlight can supply an adequate amount of vitamin B-12 but watch us for over-exposure.

- Vegetarian and vegan foods have lots of iron but don't depend solely on it if you're pregnant or still menstruating. Consider taking an Iron supplement. Watch your tea and coffee intake, and they are iron-inhibitors.

- A vegetarian diet can be perfect for you if it is well-planned and nutritionally balanced.

- Insufficient water intake will not help your body adjust to all the extra fiber it's getting from the added fruits and vegetables.

Chapter2: Why Go Vegan?

Going Vegan can benefit your health – this is probably one of the main reasons for you to go vegan because according to studies, the vegan diet can bring some advantages in the whole body. Vegans reportedly have low rates of obesity and weigh 5-20% less than those who eat meat. Vegetarian diet as a whole is linked to lower BMIs, reduced risk of cardiovascular disease (vegan diet is cholesterol free!) and type II diabetes. It can also minimize the risk of having certain cancers like colon cancer.

The benefits of going vegan are innumerable which vouches for the fact that it is indeed the best approach for a healthy and fit lifestyle. Read on to know more, and you will inevitably gear up to move forth on the path of veganism.

Reduces risk of diseases: It is the best way to make your body healthier and resistant to several ailments that come as part and parcel of modern day sedentary lifestyles. It certainly eliminates the risk of several chronic degenerative diseases such as diabetes, obesity, high blood pressure, coronary artery diseases and various types of cancer, such as colon, prostate, breast, stomach, and lung among others.

Aids weight loss: It is surely the best method not only to lose weight but it also helps you to maintain it once you have got your weight under control. Consuming too many meat and dairy products can lead to an increased accumulation of unhealthy fat and cholesterol in the body. Since this approach only allows healthy food ingredients, it ensures that your body slims down without leading to any deterioration in your health. The elimination of high fat and cholesterol related foods from your diet is an excellent way to start shedding some of the unwanted weight.

Improves Energy: It ensures higher levels of energy and boosts your immunity. The consumption of fresh fruits and vegetables acts as bowel regulator and provides regular movements. It, in turn, aids the digestive system and leaves you feeling light, active and brisk all day long.

Shuns toxic chemicals: Most often the products derived from animals such as meat and dairy products are filled with steroids, hormones and other chemical ingredients. They cause considerable damage to the body and in turn, can cause several diseases that attack your body. Sometimes it can even be fatal. Opting for vegetarian options, mainly organic foods, is the safest option.

Saves Our Environment: According to research, there is a lot of pollution and damage caused by the animal wastes, which is conveniently run into the rivers. It contaminates the drinking water and also leads to many diseases. If you decide to go for the vegan lifestyle, it also vouches for animal rights. You are not torturing them for your eating preferences, and you respect their rights to live and grow like every other living creature.

Reduces physical complaints: Studies show that people who have gone vegan have experienced a great difference in their physical health. Apart from increasing the energy levels and flushing out toxins, it also ensures healthy skin and promotes longevity of life. It helps tackle the problem of body odor, bad breath, migraines, allergies and also keep PMS symptoms at bay. It is an excellent way to ensure long tresses and healthy nails and bones.

Keep the weight off aside from losing weight since you are now off for high cholesterol diet, saturated fats, and processed food; you don't have to count calories to maintain your weight with this lifestyle. Adding exercise to your diet will also contribute to your health and fitness.

Healthy mind - according to research, vegans have lower incidences of anxiety and depression than non-vegan.

Protein deficiency is not a problem – this is one myth on vegan/vegetarian diet, and it has been proven that you'll get enough of your protein needs through a vegan diet. Furthermore, research also says that too much animal protein can be harmful to your health since it can cling as fat or strain your kidneys.

Save money – aside from eliminating some items in your closet, vegan food selection is economical. Another plus is that if you eat a well-balanced menu selection, then you don't have to buy additional supplements.

A vegan diet is yummy! –There are hundreds of recipes that are not only nutritional but delicious as well. If you think that vegan food is limited, think again. You can even have meat-like tasting veggies!

You can contribute to the environment – familiar with "change your plate, change the world" statement? It is because 20% of human-made pollutions come from the meat industry and you can do your part by not contributing to the greenhouse effect.

A vegan diet is safe – this is not a fad diet but has been around for centuries and even existed in different religious beliefs like Buddhism.

Support group – you can certainly find support groups to help you through the diet. It is a continuously growing lifestyle change. You can even find new friends!

Most often, vegans are thought of as fringe diners with an abnormal passion for promoting the rights of animals. Though it did that quite some vegans fervently support the animals, it is time for the general populace to understand that a vegan diet cum lifestyle goes further than mere animal rights.

Religiously adhering to a healthy, stable and balanced vegan regimen ensures a multitude of health values. It had also been found to be a good way to prevent some of the life-threatening diseases afflicting the people globally. Health is the usual primary reason for the shift to a regimen with few or no animal products.

Obese people and those with high cholesterol level simply have to understand the effects of animal fats in their daily food intake. But ethical issues about food protection, animal well-being, and the antibiotic defense created by feedlots are also making a vegan diet better.

The Value of the Vegan Way of Life

Most people know the advantages of eating less red meat or probably reducing whole milk consumption. A full-fledged change in lifestyle can be somewhat, if not all together, different. It should be noted that being a vegetarian does not automatically mean you are healthier or a vegan, the most vigorous of all.

There are benefits to living the vegan life:

1. Folate abounds in vegan diets. It plays a significant role in creating white and red blood cells, repairing cells, and stabilizing amino acids;

2. By lessening the amount of fat from your diet, you will improve your well-being tremendously. It is technically correct with cardiovascular wellness;

3. A vegan diet has carbohydrates which provide power for your body. A deficiency in carbohydrates will enable your body to burn your muscle tissues so that it can produce energy;

4. Due to the vegan's diet rich in fiber nature, they have healthier secretion of the body's waste matters. High fiber food also aid in the body's fight against colon cancer;

5. With nuts, dark leafy veggies and seeds, magnesium is obtained which is responsible for facilitating calcium absorption in the human body;

6. Vegan diets are usually rich in potassium which balances acidity and water in the human body. Consequently, it encourages the kidneys to get rid of toxins. High in potassium diets had been found to reduce the possibility of cancer and cardiovascular diseases;

7. Many antioxidants, which protect the cells from damage, are also found in vegan foods. Antioxidants also help in the prevention of formation of certain cancer types;

8. Plant-based diets are rich in vitamin C which boosts the immune system, helps in keeping gums healthy and bruises to heal quickly;

9. Grains, dark leafy greens, and nuts are full of vitamin E which is needed for the eyes, heart, brain, skin, and even helps in hindering the development of Alzheimer's Disease;

10. Plant-based diets are good sources of phytochemicals, which prevents and heals the body from cancer.

11. Beans, soy products, nuts, lentils, and peas are all good ways to get the right amount of protein in a vegan diet; and,

12. A vegan diet is rich in whole grains which are favorable to your health, such as prevention of Type 2 diabetes and arthritis, lowering high blood pressure, and delaying osteoporosis.

13. On top of excellent nutrition and disease restraint, vegan regimen also provides environmental values in making the body more beautiful, stronger, and full of energy.

14. Population research disclosed that a meatless diet leads to decrease in Body Mass Index, an indicator of healthy weight and decrease of fat on the body.

15. A steady reduction in pressure is a normal consequence of an appropriate vegan diet. Vegan food eliminates a significant amount of the unhealthy foodstuff that may cause weight problems.

16. The many kinds of nuts and vitamins A and E from veggies is responsible for making the skin healthy. It had been known to reduce blemishes in the skin for vegans visibly.

17. Studies conducted indicate that those on a vegan or vegetarian way of life live approximately three to six years longer than those who do not.

18. Non-consumption of red meat and dairy products had been found to decrease body odor significantly. Similarly, its effect on the smell of breath is the same. Thus, vegan means are feeling better in the body and with breath.

19. Many vegans had reported that their hair, over time, had grown stronger, healthier, glossier, and has more body.

20. Nail health is believed to be an index of overall wellness. It had been found excellent in many vegans.

21. Other benefits of veganism include:

- Helping ecology in avoiding severe bacterial contagions;

- Whether against the situations of animals for food or consuming animals in general, turning vegan will appease your conscience;

- Producing plants need fewer resources than creating animals, thus, going vegan helps lessen the toll on the ecology.

- Eating veggies completely avoid the risk of E-coli contamination, mad cow disease, and Salmonella food poisoning as its source is excluded from the vegan diet.

Chapter 3: Vegan Lifestyle: Myths and Facts

It had been estimated that there are approximately 20 million Americans who are lactovegetarians; from partial vegans who limit their meat intake; to vegans, whose diet consists of plant foods only—no meat, eggs, poultry, dairy products or fish.

All vegetarian regimen requires additional planning, and more so when you are just shifting from the regular diet meals. Just like any other diet, the crux is always in making choices. Though a vegetarian diet limits your options to a significant extent, the issue to be addressed is balancing your diet so as to maintain the required nutrients intake.

Let us take a close look at some legends enveloping vegetarian meals.

1. Myth: Vegetarian meals are all healthy.

Fact: It is relatively true that vegetarian meals are healthier as compared to the regular diet. Vegetarians have been found to have a lesser incidence of being overweight. They also have fewer chronic lingering health predicaments, like cancers, diabetes, heart disease, and high blood pressure.

It is hard to know though if this due to the diet or the whole lifestyle. Vegan lifestyle dictates having regular exercise and prohibits smoking or drinking intoxicating beverages. Besides, if you make the wrong choices on food, a vegetarian meal has also the tendency to be unhealthy.

A regular diet of French fries and ice cream sundaes, though vegetarian by nature, remains not good for the health. Some studies had also published findings that women, in general, who are vegans, may have deficiencies in vitamin B12, iron, and calcium. Due to this finding, the recommendation is eating various plant-based foods daily. Just make sure that your daily diet includes enriched whole grains, green leafy vegetables, tofu, fruits, soy milk, legumes, and beans.

2. Myth: Babies, children, and teenagers should not be allowed to be vegans.

Fact: Meeting the nutritional needs of children, infants and adolescents are still possible even though they opt to be vegans. Realistically speaking though, it will be a bit tricky to do as compared with a standard diet.

3. Myth: Pregnant and breastfeeding women should not go vegan.

Fact: You can meet the nutritional needs during the prenatal period and breastfeeding by way of a plant-based regimen if you choose astutely. Your health care provider may guide you to supplement your diet with iron, B12, or folic, as the case may be.

4. Myth: Eating a plant-based diet always decreases your risk for diseases of the heart.

Fact: Although vegans tend to have a lower possibility for heart ailments than meat-eaters, just by following a plant-based diet might be insufficient. Because of hereditary factors related to heart illnesses, a person may be susceptible to high blood pressure or high cholesterol. These considerations of risk may require treatment or medication, regardless of how heart-healthy is the food intake.

5. Myth: A vegetarian or a vegan regimen is always low fat.

Fact: If your vegetarian meals contain dairy foodstuffs, you can still have plenty of supply of fat coming from cheese, whole milk and cream. If you are a vegan, you will not consume much, if any, of animal-derived fat. You can, however, still have lots of unsaturated vegetable fat from canola and olive oil.

Although dry fat is good for the heart, it still has many calories per tablespoon as butter and can result to increase in weight if you overeat.

6. Myth: Vegans are always weak physically.

Fact: Funny but this is not true as evidenced by Carl Lewis, a star sports player, and a multiple Olympic gold medal winner. He chose to go vegan in 1990, and the next year, he had excellent results in the 1991 World Championships. Another is Mike Tyson who is also a vegan.

7. Myth: Plant-based meals are costly compared to standard meal diets.

Fact: True as natural produce comes at a bit of a higher price. But meat is one of the most expensive groceries money can buy. Thus, a vegan eats by and large at less cost

8. Myth: You easily get hungry when you are on a plant-based diet.

Fact: If you are easily hungry on a meatless diet, chances are, your food choices are wrong. It can happen when you are not getting enough protein, fiber, or fat, or protein. Fiber, the part of the plant that cannot be digested, literally makes your gut packed and stabilizes blood sugar levels, and prevents cravings.

Chapter4: The Vegan Transition

Since this is a lifestyle change, it can be hard for others to give up the food that they are used to eating. And there will be a lot of instances that you have to let go of your comfort food since it runs counter to the diet. But always keep in mind the result – a healthier you to fuel your efforts in committing to the diet.

Before sharing the tips on the vegan transition, I will first tackle the several reasons that hinder people (even the ones interested) not to pursue the diet:

Love for sweets and desserts– you can't give up your chocolates, ice cream, and cookies. These types of food usually have a huge amount of sugar, so even if you are non-vegan, you should consume this sparingly. But don't fret, you have alternatives! Try coconut/almond ice cream flavor, and there is a substitute for chocolates that taste the same. And let's not forget that the best and healthiest desserts will be fruits! And you have a variety to choose from.

Cheese - you probably think that you have to give up your pizza, burritos and the likes because of the cheese. But you can certainly train yourself; like not going to the cheese section while grocery shopping or only just plainly make it a habit not to consume cheese and you will soon find out that you are not craving for it. Habits can be changed.

Friends and family – aside from thinking that they might find you weird, you are also concerned with their reactions and might think that it would be harder for you to go out with them especially eating out. But then, friends and family will eventually be used to your lifestyle change and respect your decision especially if you explain that you are doing this for health reasons. Once they see the positive impact of your new lifestyle, you might even influence them to do the same.

Eating out you might think that restaurants are for meat-eaters, but then you might have to rethink this because all you have to do is explore your options. Research for restaurants like Indian, Japanese, Chinese and Thai restaurants in your area, plus don't be shy to ask if there are vegan options for you aside from the salads.

You don't like soy – another misconception is that vegan will require you to eat and eat lots of soy and that soy is not tasty. But you also have to know the benefits of consuming soy (reduces risk or cardiovascular diseases and can lower blood pressure) plus there are a lot of soy recipes that you can incorporate, and it tastes delicious.

Do not let others or your environment and habits hinder you from being healthy. Make a choice and stick with it. It is the first advice that I will give; you have to have a commitment to the lifestyle change for it to work.

Here are some tips to help first-time vegans:

Empty the cupboard – like in any diet; you have to get rid of anything that might tempt you. So raid your refrigerator and cupboard, get rid of all animal products (meat, dairy, eggs, and fats –yes even the butter). Canned meats or any processed food that might contain animal products has to go. You can donate the food or give it away to family and friends.

Educate yourself – aside from this book, there are also references that you can use like numerous free recipes, and nutrition info. Google is your best friend. Visit your health-care provider - before venturing to any diet, this is a must. Consult your doctor so that they can also give you basic pointers or even advise supplements in your vegan journey.

Stick to your list – forget your usual grocery route and stick to the list. You can even have a new experience by trying out specialty stores or farmer' market in your area.

Go at your pace-if you feel that you are not healthy for a full blast vegan diet, and then you can slowly transition to the diet you will also eventually develop the habit of choosing the healthier option. The sooner you can completely turn around your plate, the better.

Enjoy trying out new things make this an "exploration" or trying-something-new time for you. Discover new cuisines, let out the inner chef in you and rejoice on the conscious decision of choosing to be healthy.

Find a support group – explore the social media and you'll see that there are a lot of vegan communities that can help you out in the transition. They can even share with you vegan products recipes, restaurant tips and more. You can also ask your partner or a family member (if open) to join in your journey so that you will have an instant support system that can remind you or boost your confidence that you can do a lifestyle change.

Protein is not a problem – again, this is one of the vegan related myth or misconceptions. There are a lot of vegan alternatives like broccoli, cauliflower, asparagus, beans, soy products and more.

Find a new comfort food the vegan style – don't always try looking for a vegan substitute, since this is an "exploration time" you can try other suggested vegan comfort foods.

Don't be embarrassed with your lifestyle choice remember that you don't need to explain yourself to others. You can always stand up for your choice, and you will most likely even gain the respect of others or even influence them.

Know about faux meats and dairy alternatives since there is a lot of interest in vegan diet, and that this diet has been around for some years, there are a lot of alternative products that you can try like veggie burgers, veggie hot dogs, meatless barbecue and other vegan deli slices. For dairy products, you can try soy milk and yogurt, vegan cream cheese and even yummy non-dairy ice creams.

Have a food diary – track what you eat and weight that you have lost, this will also give you that extra inspiration that you might need to pursue the diet.

 Don't sweat if you run astray – there may be times that you might give in and eat that cheesy pizza and pasta, but instead of stressing out, repeat the process again and this time with more vengeance and extra effort.

You can join the vegan craze and be healthy! Just make that first small step, have the end goal in mind and fully commit. Before you know it, the transition is done and you will become a full-pledge vegan.

Equipping the Vegan Kitchen

The best part about converting your kitchen into a vegan kitchen is that you do not require too many types of equipment or shell out big bucks to support the lifestyle change. Load up your cutlery with some sharp knives as it greatly simplifies that work to be done. Another great tool is a mandolin, which is like a slicer and very handy for slicing ingredients. However, extreme care should be taken while handling it to prevent any damage to your hands and fingers. Another handy tool is a garlic press. Garlic acts as an excellent seasoning ingredient and adds great flavor to almost any dish and having a garlic press ready at your disposable is indeed a very good idea as it makes mincing and chopping garlic an easy task. Apart from the above-mentioned list, graters, peeler, measuring cups, spoons, and strainers come in very handy while fixing a quick meal.

Another critical kitchen equipment that every vegan should possess is a blender and a food processor. To get your healthy juices and delicious smoothies ready in a jiffy, a good quality blender works like a charm.

If you are more of a quick fixer and prefer cooking methods that require less time, then owning a pressure cooker is a must. It will soften your vegetables for a few seconds and have them imbibe the flavor very well. It takes less time and eases the cooking process. These are some of the essential equipment that you require to set up a vegan kitchen.

What to cook

Now your pantry is fully stocked and you are eager to start creating your first vegan meals! But where to start? This chapter is not a recipe book, but it is a guide that will help you find amazing recipes that are suitable for anyone, starting from the absolute beginner to the seasoned chef.

Start with the dishes you already love. If you always loved pasta with tomato sauce and rice and beans, start out with those. By starting with something familiar first, you start building your confidence and will soon be ready to try out new things.

Cook based on new ingredients. If you are using a part for the first time, search online for simple recipes that include that ingredient. If you are experimenting with quinoa, for example, look for "pure quinoa recipes" or "how to cook quinoa." This will filter out complicated dishes that might scare you, but will still allow you to get to know a new ingredient!

Buy a vegan cookbook. If you are the traditional type who loves marking their favorite recipes with bookmarks, then getting a good vegan cookbook is a worthy investment. Most of these books have precise instructions on how to prepare ingredients, make meals and even freeze them. This is why they are a good choice for people who are just starting their cooking journey, as well as for experienced cooks.

Follow vegan food blogs and websites. There you will find tons of recipes, often with step-by-step pictures of how to prepare your food. You can also join vegan social media groups and forums, where you can ask any questions concerning food preparation and what is or is not vegan. Keep in mind that discussions can get pretty heated in these forums, especially when people ask provocative questions, just to make a fuss (aka the trolls). Just ignore the negativity and focus on what you can learn about cooking.

Cook based on what travels well. If you are looking for vegan foods that you can pack and take with you at work, I have a little secret for you: look for vegan parent blogs! Vegan parents prepare the most amazing lunch boxes for their kiddos, and you can get inspired by their ideas. Just make sure to get a bigger lunchbox, since you are a big kiddo.

Explore foreign cuisines. Maybe if you are from a country or state where barbecue contests are the most popular "sport," then you will need to look elsewhere for inspiration. Mediterranean cuisine, as well as many Asian cuisines, have many dishes that are "accidentally vegan." So are many Moroccan, Algerian and Iranian dishes.

Planning for a Vegan Diet

What you are aiming for is a meatless and well balanced plant-based diet to avoid any deficiencies. The first thing that you should do is research, research and research and of course prepare your pantry.

Here are some staples for first-time vegans:

Healthy oils – go for the extra-virgin oil. You can also try canola oil and flaxseed oil as some contain an omega-3 fat that is good for your body.

Nuts and seeds for your protein requirements and healthy unsaturated fats. Nuts and seeds also contain iron, zinc and vitamin E.

Tofu – this versatile meat substitute can be one of the superstars in your kitchen. You can bake, grill, fry, and sauté your tofu! There are a lot of dishes that you can try with tofu as an ingredient.

Seasonings for a flavorful diet, you will need to stock on your seasoning. You can shop for cayenne, basil, paprika, kosher salt, curry powder, rosemary and more. You can buy this fresh at farmer's market or specialty stores.

Faux Milk – you can stock up on your whole milk substitute. You can try rice milk and almond milk. Aside from drinking it up, you can also use them for cooking and baking.

Beans-another traditional staple food for vegan since it's rich in protein and is a versatile ingredient like tofu.

Beef/Pork Substitutes – you can most likely find these veggie meats in specialty stores. Burgers anyone? You can with this vegan alternative! But note that for optimum nourishment, the non-processed vegan food is still better.

Since vegan eliminates other food groups, you have to make sure that you have a well-balanced diet and is acquiring proper nutrients to avoid any deficiencies.

Here are some vitamins nutrients that every vegan need:

Protein and Amino Acids – protein is usually associated with eating meat but also has alternative sources like eating soy while Amino Acids can be met by consuming whole grains, veggies, seeds, and nuts.

Vitamin D-if you can't get enough sunlight, you can try reliable vegan supplements.

The iron the richest source of iron is liver, egg yolk, and red meat, note that these are all high in cholesterol. To avoid iron deficiency, one can consume spinach, dried fruits, dried beans, chickpeas, pinto beans, whole wheat, parsley, fortified veggie burger, prunes, raisins and more. Another tip is to eat vitamin C rich food since it helps in iron absorption and if you're low in iron, then do not take zinc-rich food at the same meal.

Zinc-another essential nutrient for growth and development that can be found in legumes, nuts, and grains.

Omega 3-since seafood is out of the diet; you can take flax seeds/flax oil or omega 3 DHA supplements in the form of algae. It is essential especially for vegans who are breastfeeding, diabetic or pregnant (At least 300 ms of DHA a day).

Research on the best possible combination of food selection to give your body the best and complete nutrition that it can get.

How to Maintain a Vegan Diet

After the transition from being a meat-eater to a vegan eater, you will now of course stick to the lifestyle. Even as you form vegan habits, there are still pitfalls that can hinder you on your diet.

Here are some common mistakes that new vegans make and that you should avoid sticking to the diet:

Eating the same amount of food as your pre-vegan days – if you are always hungry in your new diet, then you are doing it wrong. When our are eating plant-based food, you need to eat larger portions since the calories that you are now consuming is lesser. The hunger-pangs a new vegan may feel when consuming not enough food can be one of the reasons why they try out "filling" non-vegan food again. Learn to check out calorie contents and know if you are in the right numbers.

Eating loads of processed vegan food – prepared vegan treats like veggie burgers, hot dogs, and the likes can help you stick with your no-meat policy. However, the unprocessed vegan food still offers more nutritional benefits.

Not listening to your body – as I have said, habit formation usually takes about 21 days. So let your body adjust and don't get discouraged if you are feeling a bit different or have some craving. Listen to your body carefully, if you are hungry eat if you think you are not satisfied with what you are eating, and then try out other dishes. You have to understand that your body or your system is undergoing significant changes. Another tip here is always to stay hydrated, drink up guys!

Not checking out the labels – make sure to check out the labels on some food can still contain animal products, or lactose-free labeled products are not synonymous with non-dairy products.

Getting information from not reliable sources – you might have read an article on a model sharing her vegan food plan, yes she might look good, but it does not necessarily mean that you will achieve that slim body and at the same time be healthy. Do proper research before trying out something. Again, a well-balanced diet is important.

Sticking to salad when eating out – again, you have options. You can ask the restaurant for vegan dishes, or you can search for restaurants that can fulfill your requirements.

You also have to remember that your nutrient requirements will differ when you're pregnant, lactating, or as you age. Since vegan diet is a lifestyle change (and if you decided to stick to it), then you also have to evolve depending on the situation and research more to attain the optimal nutrients for your body.

Nutrition Structure of Vegan diet

Any balanced diet requires a balance of food to manifest itself into health benefits. The nutrients listed below explain why the vegan diet is considered beneficial to the health and is easily recommended in the vegan diet plans. While it might be a bit difficult to find all sorts of nutrients in vegetables and fruits, research will give you some foods that are rich in various nutrients and still within the vegan diet restrictions.

The underlying concept of the whole vegan diet is about maximizing vitamins, fibers, magnesium, and potassium while cutting back on carbohydrates and saturated fat which can quickly become a health problem.

Fiber- Vegan diets are high in fiber, which leads to improving bowel movements, and is particularly very effective in fighting colon cancer.

Magnesium- We focus greatly on the importance of calcium in any diet and the process; we often overlook magnesium which also plays a crucial role in maintaining a balanced diet. The Vegan diet encourages consumption of nuts and seeds are particularly a good source of magnesium to the body.

Potassium- The vegan diets are high in potassium, which balances the water levels and acidity in the body, and powers the kidneys to get rid of the toxins in the body. Moreover, diets that are high in potassium are known to reduce the risk of heart diseases and even prevent cancer.

Folate-This particular vitamin plays a crucial part as it aids in cell repair, generates blood cells and even metabolizes amino acids which in turn help in digestion.

Antioxidants- Antioxidants are found in fruits and vegetables. They are undoubtedly excellent for the body and play a fundamental role by acting as a guardian against diseases. They even help prevent some types of cancer. Vitamin C which is a kind of antioxidant contributes to boosting the immune system and helps bruises to heal. Vitamin E has exceptional results on the heart, skin, and eyes and is said even to help prevent Alzheimer's disease. Moreover, the photochemical from plant-based foods will not only prevent cancer, but also has the potential to reverse the condition, and works well with the antioxidants from vegan diets.

Chapter 5: Vegetarian Diet and Weight Loss

One of the physical benefits of the vegan diet is that it is an efficient way of losing weight, as it has been mentioned in this article. Being on any diet is likely to result in some weight loss; however, vegan diet guarantees a sustainable weight loss. Alongside this, significant improvements can be noticed in cholesterol levels, blood pressure levels, blood sugar and other aspects of health.

Getting started on the vegan diet might be challenging; just the thought of following a healthy lifestyle for an indefinite period. The key principle to losing weight through vegan diet is to choose maximum foods from plant sources, of course, avoid meats and all sorts of animal products, and keep oils to the minimum.

In fact, nutritionists have come up with a nutrition chart to base vegan meals on to maximize the weight loss benefits. The model consists of four dimensions of food i.e. grains, vegetables, fruits, and sweets.

The first aspect focuses on foods and limits its intake to 80 (kcal) a day and advice that one-third of grain servings in a day should be from whole-grain sources, such as bread and brown rice. Oatmeal is a better alternative to cereals.

The second dimension is vegetables. Since vegan diets are based on vegetable consumption, there is no real limitation on their intakes. However, a dieter should have at least one serving of raw vegetables in a day whether it is in the form of salad or anything else. But the point in this is that cooked food loose most of its nutrition value, and so eating raw would give you more than two times the nutrition you get from cooked meals. Moreover, vegetables consumed in a day should contain some leafy greens and beans.

Fruits play a crucial part in the vegan diet. It mainly focuses on energizing the body and should be eaten as a whole piece to get maximum benefits instead of juicing it. Moreover, as a part of weight loss program, it would be better to go for the low-calorie fruits like strawberries, kiwis, blueberries, raspberries, and oranges since it will contradict the weight loss program if you put on weight.

The biggest difficulty that a dieter may face is that the food might not seem enough, and may often go hungry. Well, the solution to that is easy especially if you are on the vegan diet; add more vegetables and beans to your plate. And in the rare cases where the food might seem too much for you, well, it would be a better to ditch the sweets before ditching any vegetables from the meal plan.

Lastly, in the quest to lose weight most people try to cut down their calorie intakes as much as possible in a day. It isn't good in any way for your health. In fact, it may lead to nutrition deficiency in the long run. It is of utmost importance that no one, whether dieting or on regular meal plans, should ever go below the minimum standard of having at least 1200 calories a day.

Look around, and you will see that there are many different ways to lose weight. Building your meals from fruits, vegetables, whole grains, and beans is the most healthful way. It is also straightforward to do. Apart from losing weight, this type of eating improves cholesterol, blood pressure, blood sugar and many other aspects of health. The premise is simple

– cut out the foods that are high in fat and low in fiber and increase the foods that are low in fat and high in fiber. This type of diet is safe and easy to do once you have adjusted to it.

Changing your way of eating can be daunting at first. Cutting out the foods you've grown to may make you feel deprived.

To be successful in your vegetarian diet, do your best to stick to it. Begin by weighing yourself first so you can keep track of your weight loss. Keep a food journal so you can jot down your food intake. Make a note of how you feel while you're on the diet so you can monitor its effects on you.

Choose foods from plant sources and avoid all animal products. When using oil, choose vegetable oils and keep it to a bare minimum. Focus on four food groups – grains, legumes, fruits, and vegetables. These can provide you with all the nutrients you need.

The Role of Exercise Vegetarianism only has rules on animal products. A vegetarian diet can help you in weight loss and weight management if you partner it with an active lifestyle. The more exercise you do, the quicker you'll see the pounds come off. You will also reduce your risk of developing diabetes, heart problems, and other chronic diseases.

Beginning to Change

Keep in mind that it would be ideal if you could shop at farmer's markets and buy only seasonal foods, but if that is not possible, just try to purchase organic when available and to be the best "perimeter shopper" you can.

Regardless of where you shop for foods, switching to a plant-based diet is going to eliminate the "costs" of commercial growing/raising and the transportation of products. It will allow you to eat whole foods and get the most nutrients possible, and it can allow you to support a local agricultural system rather than a large commercial entity that operates far away and in ways no environmentally friendly at all.

Note: even those who decide to become "flexitarians" (semi-vegetarian) can choose seasonal and local farm goods, such as grass fed beef and cage free chickens, to ensure that the environment and the animals are not paying heavily for their consumer food choices.

Now that you know more about what you need from your foods, it is time to look at the individual food groups.

The Many Plant Based Foods

Try to make a quick list of the "plant-based foods" that you eat. You will probably mention such things as bananas, lettuce, tomatoes, and all kinds of other fruits and vegetables, but you must also add such elements as seeds and beans, nuts, grains, and everything else that provides nutrition but does not come from an animal. Those veggie burgers you enjoy or the tofu hot dogs you put on the grill in the summer are also going to fall under the heading of plant-based food as well.

It means that using this method of eating opens up your daily diet to a tremendous range of options. For example, the person on a plant-based diet could have buckwheat pancakes with blueberries for breakfast, TVP (texturized vegetable protein) chili with a corn biscuit and a green salad at lunch, a protein smoothie as an afternoon snack, and a massive pot of stir fry as their meal in the evening.

Additionally, there is always going to be the need to make that famous "rainbow on your plate" to get the calories and nutrients required, and so the many options available to the plant based eater is a real bonus.

Choosing Food

To (or "intending to") be sure you understand just how diverse your diet can be, let's look at all of the primary food sources.

Before we take a peek at the list, however; let's briefly discuss the issue of food color as mentioned above. Health advocates have said that a colorful plate is one that is well balanced regarding nutrients. Why do they say this? It is because foods contain "phytochemicals" that give them their different colors and which are the "bioactive" materials contained in the foods.

For example, we say that food has antioxidants, and what we mean is that the food is high in specific phytochemicals that are beneficial to human health and wellness.

When you eat a plant based diet, it is useful to know what the color of any particular food might mean regarding nutrition, and then try to fill your plate with as many of the beneficial compounds as possible. Below is a list of food colors and the phytochemicals that they are most known for providing.

- Pale green to white - Allicin, quercetin, and flavonoids are commonly found in foods that naturally have such hues. This group includes foods like green grapes, white grape juice, and the many kinds of onions such as leeks, chives, and even garlic.
- Green - The leafy greens are known for their indoles and sulforaphane. This group includes kale, brussels sprouts, cabbages of all kinds, and broccoli, among others.
- Yellowish Green to Bright Yellow - Containing zeaxanthin and lutein, foods in this color range include some of the greens like spinach or collard and mustard greens, but also avocados,

honeydew melon, corn on the cob, and peas of all kinds.

- Pale Yellow to Orange - This color is a good cue to high beta crypt than in content and is found in foods like peaches, oranges and orange juice, papaya, and tangerines.

- Bright Orange - The important carotenoids (what people speak about when they are discussing beta carotene as a cancer-fighting compound) are found in foods like carrots, pumpkins, mangos, cantaloupes, all of the hard-skinned squashes such as butternut and acorn, and sweet potatoes.

- Red and Purple - This is the group in which anthocyanins are found and include such richly hued foods as strawberries, grapes and grape juice, cranberries, red apples, blackberries, and even dried prunes.

Go ahead and build a rainbow on your plate during each meal, or at least try to give yourself a small sampling of these highly beneficial compounds at each mealtime. For instance, a homemade fruit smoothie that uses greens and fruits is a good way to add "color" to your plate of less interesting foods such as rice and a protein source.

Step-by-Step: Moving Toward a Plant-Based Diet

With a much clearer understanding of what it means to be a plant based eater, you can now decide how and when to make the change. We are going to provide you with some tips and tactics that can make this a much easier thing to accomplish. As we already stated, it is a good idea to make this sort of change gradually to avoid "burn out."

For example, if it is too radical of a change from the way you usually eat, you will find yourself constantly thinking, worrying, and planning. It is not something that you will sustain on a permanent basis - no one can. Thus, if you want to make the changes permanent, you have to do them slowly and in planned stages.

It is also a good idea to do this sort of change slowly because the plant-based diet is very high in fiber, and this can often lead some unsuspecting individuals to experience significant discomfort. Insoluble fiber is often a source of intestinal gas and can lead someone unused to such foods to experience bloating flatulence, and digestive trouble.

So, follow the steps and tips below, and you should be able to claim to be a plant based eater in no time!

Cut out the meat slowly - We already discussed the idea of a "meatless" day or at least one meatless meal each day, but if you are currently eating the SAD, it is likely that you are eating meat at each meal of the day. A recent article in the New York Times indicated that Americans eat an average of 200 pounds of meat per year - without adding in the dairy and the eggs. It translates to 110 grams or protein on any given day but is an amount that is twice the suggested intake. With more than 75 grams of meat or animal protein in the average diet, it can be tough just to eliminate it, but you do need to start slowly dropping consumption to around 30 grams instead.

Also, be aware of the fact that a lot of people unknowingly replace the lost protein with starchy foods to get the same feeling of "fullness." While it may seem okay to add grains or potatoes in place of a chunk of meat, it is going to give you very little nutrition and fail to provide the body with what it needs.

Instead, replace the meat with a valid protein substitute.

Eliminate dairy foods - This is often far more challenging than removing the meat. We eat dairy in ways that we may not even realize. That pat of butter on the morning toast, that dash of parmesan on the plate of pasta, or the bit of creamer in the coffee are all sources of dairy foods. Because of that, we suggest that you use the same approach to dairy elimination as used for meats.

Start with a single dairy free day each week and then gradually expand on that theme;

Start with a single dairy free meal each day, and then move on to a dairy free day;

Pick one type of dairy food, such as cheese, and eliminate that entirely from the diet over.

Find excellent substitutes and just make the switch. Soy yogurt, vegetable margarine, nut milk, and many other food choices can allow you to cut the dairy all at once. Remember, however, that cooking with these foods may require some experimentation to get the results desired. You also want to read the labels and watch the calories, fat, etc.

Cut the eggs - This is often the last big hurdle to a plant based diet. After all, eggs are such an easy and reliable food source, but the problem is that they are never an environmentally friendly or cruelty-free food source. It means that they must go! It is not something done in "stages" like so many other food sources. Instead, it is usually done by committing to an egg free diet. There are some substitutes, but many use egg whites. Read the labels and start experimenting with alternatives when baking or cooking. For example, when eggs are used in baked goods they are often meant to serve as leavening or binding, and that means that a traditional egg substitute (sold in the dairy sections of most supermarkets) will work well. If you want to make something like a quiche, however, it will require food that is close in texture to the finished product. It would be the time to experiment with tofu.

Start adding whole and unprocessed foods to the diet - If you are currently following the SAD, it means that you are probably not eating the suggested servings of fresh fruits and vegetables each day. To begin getting accustomed to the plant-based diet may be as easy as adding a small green salad, some cooked green, and red vegetables to that plate of whole wheat pasta, and shifting from processed breakfast cereals to rolled oats cooked into a sweet oatmeal. It, of course, may not be that easy because you may not be used to many of the foods considered "whole" and unprocessed.

For example, many people find tempeh, seitan, and piles of protein dense beans a bit unusual when they are suddenly used to replace a beef patty or a piece of chicken. It is also a strange experience for those used to heavily salted and roasted nuts to start eating them raw and unprocessed too.

It just means that as you remove some of the foods from your usual diet, try to find creative ways to replace them with whole and unprocessed foods. That leads us to the need to start gathering recipes, which is the next "tip."

Gather recipes, gear, and experiment in the kitchen - A lot of people who have successfully shifted from a meat eating diet to a plant based one will tell you that they had to re-learn cooking, food prep, and shopping because they were unfamiliar with the many different textures, flavors, and techniques available. This means that you should:

Find role models, inspiration, and "network connections" - In this age of the Internet you can easily find hundreds of recipes, but you can also find a lot of quick answers from food experts and enthusiasts too. Go ahead and search a place like Facebook for plant-based dieters, or the types of eaters you have chosen to become (remember that you might have opted to eat only raw foods or to eat mostly fruits, etc.). Join all of the groups that seem like a good fit and begin interacting with the community. Many of these people are happy to share recipes, resources for exotic or unusual ingredients, and to support you through your struggles when transitioning into this new lifestyle.

Shop for new gear - The plant-based diet requires a lot of chopping, slicing, and other techniques. Why not treat yourself to some excellent knives, a high-quality blender or food processor, and any other gear you have found that you need?

Expect and accept failure - Not to put a damper on your growing enthusiasm towards the plant-based diet, but you will find that there are times when it is impossible to avoid the occasional "slip" or eating the "wrong" things. Expect this, accept it, and move on.

 Everyone dives in and loves what you made, but the rest of the meal includes ample amounts of milk and some meat. You are forced, partially out of politeness and partially out of a desire to do so, to eat servings of these forbidden foods.

It is okay; don't give up your plans because of a slip. The same thing goes for the times when you are at a restaurant that is unable to accommodate your need for dairy and meat free foods. It is a matter of just doing the best that you can and continuing forward along the path to better health and an environmentally friendly lifestyle.

If you are a parent and live with other people, it is highly likely that you may be unable to recruit them into your chosen lifestyle, and that can make it very challenging. Rather than facing the risks and temptations at each meal, the savvy plant based eater plans their meals and makes a few easy to reheat selections when it is time to sit down with the rest of the family, friends, or anyone else.

That last point brings us to a very significant issue, and that is "planning." The next chapter is going to help you to succeed in making the change from the meat based eater to the plant based one. It is going to focus on the things you can do to ensure you make and eat only the healthiest, plant-based foods and meals possible.

Before we head into that section, however, let's take a moment to consider the concept of planning.

Planning to Be a Plant Based Eater

What sort of plan are we talking about here? If we are going to continue with the theme of "step by step" methods to changing the diet, we have actually to go all of the way back to the beginning. It is because you may want to create a few deadlines for your chosen goals.

Just consider that we have indicated the need to shift to one meatless day each week or one meatless meal each day. When will you begin to do this? When will you expand your efforts beyond the single day or meal? It points to the need for a calendar or a list of dates and plans. Consider the very workable template below:

1. Time to begin meatless day/meal:
2. Time to add another meatless day/meal:
3. Time to remove one type of meat from the diet:
4. Time to eliminate another meat from the diet:
5. Time to add one dairy-free day/meal:
6. Time to add another dairy-free day/meal:
7. Time to remove one type of dairy from the diet:
8. Time to eliminate another dairy from the diet:

9.   Time to remove eggs from the diet:

In addition to such simple plans, you also have to consider any of the substitutes you intend to use, when you will add more whole and unprocessed foods to the diet, what sorts of recipes you will start with, which recipes you want to use on a regular basis, and when you will shop for gear and unique ingredients.

That is a lot of planning, but it will be advantageous to you as you begin to shift into this new lifestyle. We recommend the use of a notebook or planner to help you track the dates and deadlines, to jot down notes about recipes or foods that you have liked or disliked, and to begin following your success and any challenges.

Plant Based Guidelines

We have already gone over the food groups, but to be sure you understand how to put this information to use, consider the following:

- Don't fill your plate with grains and starches. Try to cover any plate with two-thirds fruits and vegetables, and one third of protein, fat, and grains. Many folks make the mistake of filling up on starch and fat when they lose the protein, but that is a mistake. Instead, choose protein substitutes or use your veggies to "create" protein (see the last bullet point for details).
- Try to eat a rainbow and consume at least five servings of colorful fruits and vegetables every single day.
- Do eat at least six servings of grains, tubers, or legumes each day to regulate blood sugar and provide adequate energy.

- Stop buying processed foods of any kind and skip the sugar and salt.
- Remember that fruit or vegetable smoothies and shakes are a straightforward and filling way to get your necessary nutrients, fiber, and food.
- Combine foods to create enough protein and fat combinations. For example, a salad or side dish that uses green beans, barley, and almonds makes a complete protein! To help with this issue we provide a table below, but it is enough easy to find your favorite combinations by experimenting over time.

It is that simple, but you do have to start to think like an artist and have the necessary materials at hand to begin making your masterpieces of nutrition. Before we head to the regular shopping list, let's take a moment to explore those protein combinations.

Chapter6: Tips for Vegan Dieting

Just including vegan foods in your diet is bound to bring you astounding health benefits, however here are a few tips that will help you maximize the health benefits.

First and foremost, when shopping for ingredients, do take the time to check the labels of the packaged foods that you plan to prepare. This is because unhealthy condiments would lower the vegan quality of your meal.

We should also be aware of the contents when buying foods derived from dairy products. Cooking with milk products would ruin the entire concept of vegan eating. Moreover, be cautious of non-vegan wines as they are often processed with animal products. Also, remember that most bread and bakery foods contain some level of butter and milk.

Dealing with social pressure

When you decide to go vegan, it is wise to keep it to yourself at first, until you are confident about your diet and also about the reasons why you decided to go vegan. Once you start announcing this change to your social circle, you will realize that some people become defensive. You might be saying "I went vegan," but all they hear is "Why are you not going vegan, too?!".

The truth is that we all know deep inside that the standard western diet is destroying our health and the planet and whenever someone decides to go vegan, they remind the rest of the world of this fact. So, in order not to change their crappy diets, people just choose to treat the vegans as if they are the crazy ones.

Be calm but firm. If people attack you, by telling you that what you do is unhealthy, extreme or downright stupid, just tell them that you appreciate their concern, but you have done your research and felt that it is best for you.

Be flexible, when going out. Don't be grumpy all the time about the lack of vegan restaurants and vegan options. We usually go out to enjoy the company of friends and family. If the food is great, even better. But don't make a fuss about it. Even the most hard-core steak house will be able to offer you a gorgeous salad or a simple pasta dish if you ask nicely. Hopefully, if you have a positive attitude, in the long run, your friends will follow you to a vegan restaurant.

Cook delicious vegan food. When invited to dinners and parties, offer to bring a dish for everyone to share. This way you can a) prove how sublime vegan food can be and b) make sure that there will be something you can eat.

If attacked, leave. Unfortunately, there are still people living among us who cannot respect other people's lifestyle and choices. Such people might try to irritate, provoke and offend you. You do not have anything to prove to these people, whose minds are even more closed than their ears. You do not have to make a big scene while leaving. Just pick up your bag and go, after saying goodbye to the rest of the company. After all, you are not the immature one here.

Chapter7: Menu suggestions and recipes to get started

This is a suggested daily meal plan if you want to lose weight via a vegetarian diet.

Breakfast

- Poached egg and tomato on toast - 195 calories
- Cream cheese and tomato bagel - 250 calories
- Shredded wheat and banana - 255 calories
- Bran flakes and fruit – 255 calories
- Fruity muesli – 260 calories
- Milkshake and fruit salad – 260 calories
- Scrambled eggs on toast – 280 calories
- Toast and peanut butter – 285 calories
- Fruit salad with yogurt and oats – 345 calories
- Beans, mushrooms, and tomatoes on toast – 380 calories

Lunch

- Jacket potato with cottage cheese – 295 calories
- Hummus, crudités, and pita – 300 calories
- Tropical fruit salad – 330 calories
- Egg mayo and tomato sandwich – 340 calories
- Italian salad – 345 calories
- Lentil soup and oatcakes – 355 calories

- Greek salad wrap – 365 calories
- Beans and cheese on toast – 370 calories
- Cottage cheese and avocado on rye – 385 calories
- Mixed bean salad – 435 calories

Dinner

- Creamy mushroom pasta – 285 calories
- Veggie stir fry with rice – 390 calories
- Roasted vegetables – 380 calories
- Stuffed peppers – 425 calories
- Jacket potato with cheese and beans – 440 calories
- Moroccan salad – 465 calories
- Cheese omelet – 510 calories
- Veggie fajitas – 515 calories
- Egg Florentine – 515 calories
- Vegetable chili – 530 calories

Snacks

- Healthy fruit pavlova – 100 calories
- Pitta and salad – 160 calories
- Fruit salad and yogurt – 165 calories
- Vegetable soup and toast – 175 calories
- Sunflower seeds – 185 calories
- Nuts – 195 calories
- Bran flakes with milk – 225 calories

RECIPES

BREAKFAST

1. Breakfast Banana Bread

Preparation time: 35 minutes

Serves: 6

Ingredients:

- 1 ½ cups organic all-purpose flour
- 1/3 cup coconut sugar
- 1 ½ tsp baking powder
- Four ripe bananas (peeled)
- 3 tbsp. chopped walnuts
- ¼ cup coconut oil
- Salt to taste
- A pinch of nutmeg

Preparations:

1. Preheat oven at 350 °F.
2. In a bowl, mix flour, baking powder, nutmeg, and salt.

3. Mash bananas until no chunks are visible. Pour in sugar and oil into mashed bananas and mix ingredients together.

4. Fold in your dry ingredients with your banana mixture and chopped walnuts.

5. When cooled, let it cool for a few moments before serving. Alternatively, you may store your bread in an airtight container to keep it fresh.

Nutritional Information per serving

Total calories: 271

Protein: 8

Carbs: 47

Fiber: 3.25

Fat: 6

2. French Toast with Cinnamon

This dish is sure to delight the whole family. It will warm you from the inside out and every bite

Preparation time: 30 minutes

Serves: 6

Ingredients:

- ¾ cup unsweetened vanilla almond milk

- One tsp vanilla

- Two ripe bananas

- Six slices of toast

- 2-3 tbsp. vegan butter

- ½ tsp cinnamon

- ¼ tsp allspice

- Your favorite topping

Preparations:

1. Using a food processor, blend bananas, almond milk, cinnamon, allspice and vanilla until a thick paste is formed. Take out the mixture in a thick plate.
2. Dip toast in the blend from both sides.
3. Melt butter in a skillet while on medium heat. When butter has melted, place your dipped slice in and let

it cook for around 2-3 minutes on each side or until golden.

4. When your entire batch is complete, top it off with your favorite French toast topping or just add in a little more cinnamon.

Nutritional Information per serving

Total calories: 260

Protein: 7

Carbs: 49

Fiber: 1.25

Fat: 5

LUNCH

3. Bean and Corn Enchiladas

The dish is delicious and will please anyone's appetite

Preparation time: 15minutes

Serves: 5

Ingredients:

- One can black beans
- 1 ½ cup corn
- 1 cup vegan cream cheese
- 2/3 cup vegan cheddar (grated)
- 4 tbsp. canned jalapeno
- 2 tbsp. juice from canned jalapeno
- 12 corn tortillas
- Coconut oil
- Sauce ingredients:
- 2 cups tomato sauce
- ½ cup vegetable broth
- One tsp chili powder
- One tsp garlic powder
- One tsp cumin powder
- One tsp oregano
- One tsp onion powder

Preparations:

1. Preheat oven to 350 degrees.
2. Cook black beans, jalapeño, jalapeño juice and corn over medium heat in skillet laced with coconut oil.
3. Once beans are cooked, drain the remaining liquid.
4. Add all sauce ingredients into a saucepan and cook over medium heat for 3-5 minutes.
5. Spread sauce on your baking sheet and place tortilla. Smear vegan cream cheese on each tortilla before adding a few tbsp. Of your bean and corn mix on top.
6. Roll tortillas and add a little sauce on top before placing the dish into your oven for around 20 minutes.
7. Cool before serving.

Nutritional Information per serving

Total calories: 260

Protein: 5

Carbs: 40

Fiber: 1.34

Fat: 5

4. Raw Taco Wrap

Now you can enjoy them all together in soup that is just as delicious as each food.

Preparation time: 35 minutes

Serves: 6

Ingredients:

- 3 Tomatoes (chopped)

- One butter lettuce

- ½ Avocado

- 1½ cups walnuts

- 1½ cups blanched almonds

- 2 tbsp. ground cumin

- One tsp garlic powder

- One tsp onion powder

- 1 tsp chili powder

- ½ bunch cilantro (finely chopped)

- Salt and ground black pepper to taste

Preparations:

1. Blend walnuts, spices and almonds in a blender and pulse until minced.

2. . Scoop avocado pit and slice the flesh into eight wedges.

3. Pick lettuce for around eight leaves to use as tacos.

4. Add nut mix onto the lettuce leaf and avocado wedge before serving.

Nutritional Information per serving

Total calories: 271

Protein: 8

Carbs: 47

Fiber: 3.25

Fat: 6

DINNER

5. Perfectly Vegan Spaghetti

It makes for the perfect meal to serve up whenever you want to spoil yourself truly.

Serves: 4-5

Ingredients:

- One large spaghetti squash

- Basil

- Garlic powder

- One tablespoon coconut cream

- 1 cup water

- Dash of Pink Himalayan Sea Salt

Directions:

1. Keep the open sides facing up as you do this; you may have to stack one on top of the other to ensure that they fit into the pan.

2. Add the water and other ingredients into the water, around the base of your squash.

3. Release the lid on the pressure cooker, then pull the squash out. Scoop out the center, then add the centers alone back into the pressure cooker, and swirl around with the other ingredients.

4. Serve immediately.

6. Very Vegan Tomato Soup

It is easy to make, and once your guests get a taste of it.

Serves: 4

Ingredients:

- Two cans diced tomatoes

- One can full-fat coconut cream

- One large can tomato sauce (original)

- One tablespoon Basil

- Two cloves garlic

- Salt and pepper to taste

- 1 cup coconut milk (original)

Directions:

1. Open and drain the cans of diced tomatoes, and combine all ingredients in the pressure cooker.

2. Turn the pressure cooker onto high pressure, and cook at high pressure for roughly 3 minutes.

3. Release the pressure, give the ingredients a good stir, and serve immediately.

SNACKS

7. Roasted Mixed Nuts

It's a delicious snack you need to try soon!

Serves: 24

Time: 10 minutes

Ingredients:

- 4 cups pecans
- 2 cups almonds
- 1 cup hazelnuts
- Six tablespoons agave nectar
- ½ cup sugar in the raw
- Cinnamon

Directions:

- Preheat your instant pot to medium heat, and mix your nuts together in another dish.
- Combine the sugar with the agave nectar, then coat your balls with the mix.
- Place in your instant pot, and cover with the lid. Cook on low pressure for 20 minutes, then spread on a baking sheet covered with parchment paper to set up.
- Store in the fridge.

Nutritional information

Total calories: 336

Protein: 5

Carbs: 49

Fiber: 7

Fat: 14

8. Spicy Zucchini Bites

It's not only incredibly tasty! It is also easy to make.

Serves: 24

Time: 15 minutes

Ingredients:

- Three large zucchini
- One teaspoon cayenne pepper
- One tablespoon red pepper flakes
- Coconut oil
- Paprika
- Salt and pepper to taste

Directions:

- Slice your zucchini slices into coins. Not super thin, but not overly thick, either.
- Line the bottom of your pot with zucchini slices, then drizzle some coconut oil and add seasoning in next.
- Repeat this process until you run out of zucchini slices.
- Seal with the lid, then turn your pressure cooker on to high pressure.
- Serve with little toothpicks.

Nutritional information

Total calories: 336

Protein: 5

Carbs: 49

Fiber: 7

Fat: 14

DESSERTS

9. Banana Bread

It is a recipe that you can make whenever you are looking for something on the filling side that has a bit of an exotic taste.

Preparation time: 40 minutes

Serves: 5

Ingredients:

1/2 tsp apple cider vinegar

1/2 cup whole wheat flour

1 1/2 cup flour

One tsp vanilla

1/2 cup vegan butter

1 cup brown sugar

Three mashed bananas

One tsp baking powder

1/2 tsp baking soda

1/4 tsp nutmeg

1/4 tsp salt

3/4 cup toasted and chopped walnuts

Preparations:

1. Preheat oven to 350F
2. Grease and flour a 9" loaf pan
3. Add vinegar to the vegan milk in a small bowl and stir
4. Mix the vegan butter and sugar in a large bowl
5. Add the milk mixture, along with the bananas and vanilla to the large bowl and mix well
6. Mix flours, baking soda, baking powder, nutmeg, and salt in another bowl
7. Add mixture to the large bowl and beat well
8. Add walnuts
9. Check if bread is done by inserting a toothpick near the center of the loaf If it comes out mostly clean then the loaf is done
10. Cool for ten minutes in the pan, then place on dish and let it cool thoroughly

Nutritional Information per serving

Total calories: 190

Protein: 7

Carbs: 40

Fiber: 3.25

Fat: 6

10. Carrot Cake with cream cheese frosting

It makes for the perfect appetizer to serve up whenever you want to spoil yourself truly.

Preparation time: 35 minutes

Serves: 6

Ingredients:

- For cake:
- 3/4 cup brown sugar
- 1/2 cup chopped walnuts
- 1/2 tsp allspice
- 1/4 tsp salt
- One tsp vanilla extract
- 3 tbsp. safflower oil
- 1/4 cup almond milk, unsweetened
- 1 cup shredded carrots

- For frosting:
- 1 cup of tofu cream cheese
- 1/2 tsp vanilla extract
- Two tsp agave syrup

Preparations:

For cake:

1. Preheat oven to 350 F
2. Mix whole wheat flour, brown sugar, cinnamon, baking soda, baking powder, allspice, walnuts and salt in a large mixing bowl and mix well
3. Pour the almond milk into another separate mixing bowl and add vanilla extract, safflower oil, grated carrots and mix well
4. Add almond milk mixture to the other mixing bowl
5. Mix well and pour into a 9x9 round cake pan
6. Set cake to cool

For frosting:

1. Combine all ingredients in a mixing bowl
2. Mix well
3. Apply to cake once cake is cooled

Nutritional Information per serving

Total calories: 271

Protein: 8

Carbs: 47

Fiber: 3.25

Fat: 6

CONCLUSION

Thank you again for downloading this book!

The clamor for healthy foods has led to an increase in the number of people who are vegetarians, most of who react to the growing concerns about the environment, animal preservation, and ethical issues. Some even choose to avoid dairy products and meat because of ethical reasons associated with how they are prepared. Most of them chose the vegan lifestyle so as to help control cholesterol and reduce weight. However, other than considering these factors, being vegan is healthy and a right approach to dieting and keeping fit.

Vegan diet is indeed good for your health. In addition to physical benefits like boosting stamina and aiding in weight loss, the vegan diet gives extraordinary results in helping prevent diseases like cardiovascular complications, cholesterol, blood pressure and type 2-diabetes. It is even useful in managing ailments such prostate cancer, colon cancer, and breast cancer. Therefore, a vegetarian lifestyle helps one to lead a healthier lifestyle and live longer.

As a result, we should value the vegan diet based on its nutrition structure, obvious health benefits, and its ability to prevent diseases. You can also rate it based on its capacity in helping preserve animal rights and other ethical norms. It is undoubtedly beneficial for people who suffer from heart disease, cholesterol, and blood pressure issues. Also, it can be advantageous if it can be used to fight cancer.

Do you need any more reasons for choosing right?!..

Lastly, if you enjoyed this book and found it useful, **please** leave a review on Amazon

I would really appreciate that, your support really does make a difference and I read all the reviews personally so I can get your feedback and make this book even better.

Thanks again for your support!

Here's to being the healthy and happy person you were always meant to be!

Made in the USA
Middletown, DE
01 October 2017